Twenty to Make

Crocheted Granny Squares

Val Pierce

Search Press

First published in Great Britain 2012

Search Press Limited
Wellwood, North Farm Road,
Tunbridge Wells, Kent TN2 3DR

Text copyright © Val Pierce 2012

Photographs by Debbie Patterson at
Search Press Studios

Photographs and design copyright
© Search Press Ltd 2012

ISBN 978 1 84448 819 3

Suppliers
If you have difficulty in obtaining any of the
materials and equipment mentioned in this book,
then please visit the Search Press website for
details of suppliers: www.searchpress.com

Printed in Malaysia

Dedication
*I dedicate this book to grannies
everywhere – without whose
diligence in passing down their skills
and expertise over the years, these
delightful squares would never have
come into existence.*

Contents

The hand warmers shown opposite were based on the Tudor Rose design above (see page 24).

Introduction

If you want to learn how to crochet, what better way than to make a granny square. The simple techniques have lasted for decades and now the humble granny square is making a comeback. Now even trendier than ever, and with endless colour and size variations, creating these hip little squares is lots of fun and very, very easy.

Used like building blocks, granny squares can be stitched or crocheted together to make gorgeous gifts, accessories and items for the home, or used on their own to embellish larger items. Each square takes only a few hours to make, and along with your hook and yarn will fit easily into a small bag, making it highly portable. Take your project with you when you go out and work on it whenever you have a few minutes to spare – you will soon have enough squares to make a stunning throw for a bed or sofa that is totally unique and will last a lifetime.

In this book I will show you how to create 20 different granny squares, including flower patterns, circles, hexagons and triangles, all interpreted in different colours to create a kaleidoscope of effects. Also included are eight projects that show you how to make your squares into a pretty baby blanket, a pair of arm warmers, a gorgeous scarf, a vintage-style shoulder bag, a floral mat, a pincushion, a dainty mug cosy and a lacy cushion cover. DMC yarns have been used to create the granny squares, but various other knitting yarns have been used for the projects to demonstrate their amazing versatility. Experiment with different yarns and colour combinations, and you will soon be hooked.

Happy crocheting to you all!

Hints and tips

American and British crochet terminology
In all the patterns, US terms are given first, followed by the UK terms afterwards in brackets. So US single crochet would be written as sc (*UKdc*) and US double crochet as dc (*UKtr*).

Techniques
The first pattern in this book is the traditional granny square. It is very simple to make and perfect for learning the art of crochet.

For all the granny squares, DMC Petra 3 crochet cotton and a 3.00mm (US D, UK 10) crochet hook have been used. You can, however, replace crochet cotton with an equivalent fingering (4-ply) yarn. For the projects, various knitting yarns have been used.

Granny squares can be made in most weights of yarn, though you will need to vary the hook size to accommodate the thickness of the yarn: use hook size 3.00mm (US D, UK 10) with Petra 3 crochet cotton and fingering (4-ply) yarn; hook size 4.00mm (US G, UK 8) with double knitting (8-ply) yarn; and hook size 4.5mm (US G, UK 7) with aran weight (10-ply) yarns. As you progress to more bulky yarns then the hook you use obviously needs to be larger.

Note: the US and UK hook sizes given in this book are for guidance only, as there is no precise correspondence between the two. All the US and UK hook sizes given refer to aluminium or plastic hooks; steel hooks are generally smaller than those used in this book.

Various yarns have been used for the projects, but these can, of course, be varied depending on your personal choice or what you have available in your stash. It is advisable to keep to the same weight of yarn within each project so that the squares are a uniform size.

Although squares are simple and quick to create, working in the hundreds of yarn ends resulting from many colour changes can prove very time consuming when making up the projects. Wherever possible, crochet over the yarn ends as you make the squares, but I find that it also works well if you make a certain number of squares then work in all the ends before continuing with the next batch.

Measurements
The dimensions of each granny square are provided with the patterns.

The most frequently used terms in this book are:

American	British
slip stitch (sl st)	slip stitch (sl st)
chain stitch (ch)	chain stitch (ch)
chain space (ch sp)	chain space (ch sp)
single crochet (sc)	double crochet (dc)
half double crochet (hdc)	half treble crochet (htr)
double crochet (dc)	treble crochet (tr)
treble crochet (tr)	double treble crochet (dtr)
double treble crochet (dtr)	triple treble crochet (trtr)
skip	miss
yarn round hook (yrh)	yarn round hook (yrh)
beginning (beg)	beginning (beg)
repeat (rep)	repeat (rep)
space (sp)	space (sp)

Traditional Granny Square

Materials and equipment:

Crochet hook size 3.00mm (US D, UK 10)

DMC Petra 3 crochet cotton – small amounts
  in each of 4 colours: A, B, C and D.
  Alternatively, 1 x 50g ball in each colour will
  make several squares.

Motif size:

3in (7.5cm) diameter

Instructions:

Using A, make 6 ch, join into a circle with a sl st.

Round 1: using A, 3 ch, 2 dc (*UKtr*) into ring, 2 ch, 3 dc (*UKtr*) into
ring, 2 ch, 3 dc (*UKtr*) into ring, 2 ch, 3 dc (*UKtr*) into ring, 2 ch,
join with a sl st to top of 3 ch at beg of round. Fasten off. You will
now have 4 corner sp. Break A.

Round 2: using B, join to any corner with a sl st, 3 ch, 2 dc (*UKtr*),
2 ch, 3 dc (*UKtr*) into same corner sp, *2 ch, 3 dc (*UKtr*), 2 ch, 3 dc
(*UKtr*) into next corner sp*, rep from * to * all round ending 2 ch,
sl st to top of 3 ch at beg of round. Fasten off. You will now have
4 corner sp and one 2 ch sp between each corner. Break B.

Round 3: using C, join to any corner sp with a sl st, 3 ch, 2 dc
(*UKtr*), 2 ch, 3 dc (*UKtr*) into same corner sp, *2 ch, 3 dc (*UKtr*)
into next 2 ch sp, 2 ch, 3 dc (*UKtr*), 2 ch, 3 dc (*UKtr*) into next
corner sp*, rep from * to * all round ending last rep with 2 ch,
3 dc (*UKtr*) into next 2 ch sp, 2 ch, sl st to top of 3 ch at beg of
round. Fasten off. You will now have 4 corner sp, with two 2 ch sp
between each corner. Break C.

Round 4: using D, work as for round 3, adding an extra 2 ch sp
between the corners and working 3 dc (*UKtr*) into the sp made.
Fasten off and work in all the ends.

Poppies & Daisies

Materials and equipment:

Crochet hook size 3.00mm (US D, UK 10)

DMC Petra 3 crochet cotton – small amounts in each of 4 colours: A, B, C and D. Alternatively, 1 x 50g ball in each colour will make several squares.

Motif size:

3½in (9cm) diameter

Special abbreviations:

5 dc (*UKtr*) cluster: work 5 dc (*UKtr*) into next sp keeping last loop of each dc (*UKtr*) on hook, yrh, draw through all loops on hook.

Long dc (*UKtr*): work dc (*UKtr*) as normal but pull up a longer loop of yarn as you do so.

Instructions:

Using A, 6 ch, join into a circle with a sl st.

Round 1: 5 ch [counts as first dc (*UKtr*) and ch sp], *1 dc (*UKtr*) into circle, 2 ch*, rep from * to * 6 more times, join with sl st to 3rd of 5 ch at beg of round (8 x 2 ch sp). Break A.

Round 2: using B, sl st into first 2 ch sp, 3 ch, work 4 dc (*UKtr*) into sp but keeping last loop of each dc (*UKtr*) on hook, yrh, draw through all loops on hook [5 dc (*UKtr*) cluster made], 4 ch, *5 dc (*UKtr*) cluster in next sp, 4 ch*, rep from * to * all round, join with a sl st to top of first cluster at beg of round. Break B.

Round 3: using C, 1 ch, 1 sc (*UKdc*) into top of cluster, *3 ch, 1 long dc (*UKtr*) into top of dc (*UKtr*) on 2nd round, 3 ch, 1 sc (*UKdc*) into top of next 5 dc (*UKtr*) cluster*, rep from * to * all round, ending 3 ch, sl st to top of 5 dc (*UKtr*) cluster at beg of round. Break C.

Round 4: using D, sl st into first 3 ch sp, 3 ch, [3 dc (*UKtr*), 3 ch, 4 dc (*UKtr*)] into same sp, *3 dc (*UKtr*) into each of next three 3 ch sp, [(4 dc (*UKtr*), 3 ch, 4 dc (*UKtr*)] into next 3 ch sp*, rep from * to * twice more, 3 dc (*UKtr*) into each of next three 3 ch sp, sl st into top of 3 ch at beg of round. Fasten off.

Work in all the ends.

Square Dance

Materials and equipment:

Crochet hook size 3.00mm (US D, UK 10)

DMC Petra 3 crochet cotton – small amounts in each of 3 colours A, B and C.

For the vase cover:

DMC Petra 3 crochet cotton – small amounts in each of 3 colours A, B and C (enough to make 3 motifs)

2 small matching buttons

Matching thread and sewing needle

Motif size:

2¼in (6cm) diameter

Instructions:

Using A, make 8 ch, join into a ring with a sl st.

Round 1: work 1 ch, 12 sc (*UKdc*) into a ring, join with a sl st.

Round 2: 3 ch, 1 dc (*UKtr*) into same sp as 3 ch, 2 dc (*UKtr*) into each sc (*UKdc*) to end, join to 3 ch at beg of round, 24 dc (*UKtr*). Break A.

Round 3: using B, work 4 ch, miss 2 dc (*UKtr*), 1 dc (*UKtr*) into sp, 1 ch, miss 2 dc (*UKtr*), **7 dc (*UKtr*) into next sp, *1 ch, miss 2 dc (*UKtr*), 1 dc (*UKtr*) into sp between next 2 dc (*UKtr*)*, rep from * to * once more, 1 ch, miss 2 dc (*UKtr*)**, rep from ** to ** twice more, 6 dc (*UKtr*) into same sp as 4 ch at beg of round, join with a sl st to 3rd of 4 ch. Break B.

Round 4: using C, ***[*1 ch, 1 sc (*UKdc*) in next sp*, rep from * to * twice more, 1 ch, miss 3 dc (*UKtr*), 9 dc (*UKtr*) in next dc (*UKtr*), miss 3 dc (*UKtr*)]**, rep from ** to ** 3 more times, join with a sl st to beg of round. Fasten off and work in all the ends.

To make the vase cover:

1 Make three motifs, either in the same or different colours. Sew them together in a strip.

2 Working along one short end, rejoin the yarn and work 15 sc (*UKdc*) all along the edge.

3 Turn and work a further two rows of sc (*UKdc*). Fasten off.

4 Work along the other short end in the same way, but on the second row work a buttonhole at either end as follow: work 2 sc (*UKdc*), 3 ch, miss 1 sc (*UKdc*), work in dc (*UKtr*) to last 3 sc (*UKdc*), 3 ch, miss 1 sc (*UKdc*), 1 sc (*UKdc*) in each of last 2 sc (*UKdc*). Fasten off.

5 Sew in the ends and attach buttons to correspond with the buttonholes.

*Use this pretty vase cover to decorate candle
holders, flower holders and drinking glasses.*

Daffodil Square

Materials and equipment:

Crochet hook size 3.00mm (US D, UK 10)

DMC Petra 3 crochet cotton – small amounts
in each of 4 colours: A, B, C and D.
Alternatively, 1 x 50g ball in each colour will
make several squares.

Motif size:

3in (7.5cm) diameter

Instructions:

Using A, 8 ch, join with a sl st into a circle.

Round 1: 1 ch, work 16 sc (*UKdc*) into ring, join as before.
Break A.

Round 2: using B, 3 ch, 2 dc (*UKtr*) into same st, leaving last loop
of each dc (*UKtr*) on hook, yrh and draw yarn through all loops
on hook, *2 ch, miss 1 sc (*UKdc*), 3 dc (*UKtr*) into next sc (*UKdc*)
leaving last loop of each st on hook, yrh, draw yarn through all
loops*, rep from * to * all round, ending last rep with 2 ch, miss 1
sc (*UKdc*), sl st to top of 3 ch at beg of round. Break B.

Round 3: using C, sl st into first 2 ch sp, 3 ch, 3 dc (*UKtr*) into
same sp, *3 ch, 4 dc (*UKtr*) into next 2 ch sp*, rep from * to * all
round, ending last rep with 3 ch, join with a sl st to top of 3 ch at
beg of round. Break C.

Round 4: sl st to first 3 ch sp. Using D, [3 ch, 4 dc (*UKtr*), 2 ch, 5
dc (*UKtr*)] into same sp, *4 dc (*UKtr*) into next sp, [5 dc (*UKtr*), 2
ch, 5 dc (*UKtr*)] into next sp*, rep from * to * all round, sl st to top
of 3 ch at beg of round. Fasten off and work in all the ends.

Twisted Treble Hexagon

Materials and equipment:

Crochet hook size 3.00mm (US D, UK 10)

DMC Petra 3 crochet cotton – small amounts in
each of 3 colours: A, B and C.
Alternatively, 1 x 50g ball in each
colour will make several
hexagons.

Motif size:

3¼in (8cm) diameter

Instructions:

Using A, make 8 ch, join into a circle with a sl st.

Round 1: 3 ch, 23 dc (*UKtr*) into ring, join with a sl st to top of 3 ch at
beg of round [24 dc (*UKtr*)].

Round 2: 3 ch, 1 dc (*UKtr*) into each of next 3 dc (*UKtr*), *3 ch, 1 dc
(*UKtr*) into each of next 4 dc (*UKtr*)*, rep from * to * 4 more times,
ending last rep with 3 ch, sl st to top of 3 ch at beg of round.
Break A.

Round 3: using B, 3 ch, 1 dc (*UKtr*) into each of next 3 dc (*UKtr*), *1
dc (*UKtr*), 3 ch,1 dc (*UKtr*) into next sp, 1 dc (*UKtr*) into each of next 4
dc (*UKtr*)*, rep from * to * all round, ending last rep with 1 dc (*UKtr*),
3 ch,1 dc (*UKtr*) into next sp, sl st to top of 3 ch at beg of round.
Break B. Turn and work next row from wrong side as follows:

Round 4: using C, sl st into next sp, 6 ch, *[1 dc (*UKtr*) round stem
of dc (*UKtr*) of previous row, inserting hook from front to back*, rep
from * to * 5 more times, 3 ch]**, rep from * to ** 5 more times, sl st
to top of 3rd ch at beg of round. Fasten off and work in all the ends.

Cappuccino Lace Square

Materials and equipment:

Crochet hook size 3.00mm (US D, UK 10)

DMC Petra 3 crochet cotton – small amounts in each of 3 colours A, B and C

For the cushion:

Crochet hook size 3.75mm (US F, UK 9)

DMC Petra 3 crochet cotton – small amounts in each of 3 colours A, B and C

Cushion pad, 10 x 17in (25.5 x 43cm)

Gauge/tension for pattern on back: 17 dc (UKtr) x 9 rows = 4in (10cm)

Motif size:

3in (7.5cm) diameter

Instructions:

Using A, make 10 ch, join into a circle with a sl st.

Round 1: 3 ch, work 31 dc (UKtr) into circle, join with a sl st to top of 3 ch at beg of round [32 dc (UKtr)].

Round 2: 1 sc (UKdc) into same sp as join, *7 ch, miss 3 sc (UKdc), 1sc (UKdc) into next sc (UKdc)*, rep from * to * all round, work last sc (UKdc) into same sp as join of previous round. Break A.

Round 3: using B, sl st to 4th ch of first 7 ch sp, 3 ch, 2 dc (UKtr) into same sp but leave last loop of each st on hook, yrh, draw loop through, 3 ch, 3 dc (UKtr) into same st, leaving last loop of each st on hook, yrh and draw through all loops (cluster made), *3 ch into 4th ch of next 7 ch loops, cluster, 3 ch, cluster*, rep from * to * all round, ending last rep with 3 ch, sl st to top of 3 ch at beg of round. Break B.

Round 4: using C, 3 dc (UKtr), 3 ch, 3 dc (UKtr) into first 3 ch sp, *2 ch, 1 sc (UKdc) into next sp, 2 ch, 1 sc (UKdc) into next sp**, 3 dc (UKtr), 3 ch, 3 dc (UKtr) into next sp*, rep from * to * all round ending last rep at **, sl st to top of 3 ch at beg of round. Fasten off and work in all the ends.

To make the cushion:

Make 8 squares, 4 as described in the pattern and 4 swapping yarns A and B. Work in the ends and join the squares together in 2 rows of 4 squares, alternating the colours as shown.

Join yarn C to any corner and proceed to work around the entire perimeter of the cushion as follows:

Round 1: 3 ch,1 dc (UKtr), 2 ch, 2 dc (UKtr) into same corner sp, now work along the top of each square, working 1 dc (*UKtr*) into each dc (*UKtr*) and sc (*UKdc*) and 2 sc (*UKdc*) into each sp, to first corner, work 2 dc (*UKtr*), 3 ch, 2 dc (*UKtr*) into corner sp, continue in the same way all around the cushion front, joining with a sl st to the top of 3 ch at beg of round.

Round 2: 3 ch, 1 dc (*UKtr*) into next dc (*UKtr*), 3 ch, 2 dc (*UKtr*) into corner sp, continue to work 1 dc (*UKtr*) into each dc (*UKtr*) all round the piece, working 2 dc (*UKtr*), 3 ch, 2 dc (*UKtr*) into each corner sp, join as before. Fasten off.

Back:
Using a 3.75mm (US F/5, UK 9) hook and C, make 44 ch, 1 dc (*UKtr*) into 3rd ch from hook, 1 dc (*UKtr*) into each ch to end, turn [42 dc (*UKtr*)].

Row 1: *3 ch, 1 dc (*UKtr*) into next dc (*UKtr*), miss 1 dc (*UKtr*), 1 dc (*UKtr*) in next dc (*UKtr*), 1 dc (*UKtr*) into missed st*, rep from * to * all across row, ending 1 dc (*UKtr*) into each of last 2 dc (*UKtr*), turn.

Row 2: 3 ch, 1 dc (*UKtr*) into each dc (*UKtr*) across row, turn.

These 2 rows form the pattern and are repeated.

Continue in pattern until work is the same length as the front. Fasten off.

Work in all the ends. Join the back of the cushion cover to the front, leaving a gap for the cushion pad, insert the pad and close up.

Nursery Granny Square

Materials and equipment:

Crochet hook size 3.00mm (US D, UK 10)

DMC Petra 3 crochet cotton – small amounts in each of 3 colours: A, B and C. Alternatively, 1 x 50g ball in each colour will make several of these squares.

Motif size:

3½in (9cm) diameter

Instructions:

Using A, make 4 ch, join into a ring with a sl st.

Round 1: 3 ch, 2 dc (*UKtr*) into ring, leaving last loop of each dc (*UKtr*) on hook, yrh, draw yarn through all loops on hook, *3 ch, 3 dc (*UKtr*) into ring, leaving last loop of each dc (*UKtr*) on hook, yrh, draw yarn through all loops*, rep from * to * twice more, 3 ch, join with a sl st to top of 3 ch at beg of round. Break A.

Round 2: using B, sl st into next 3 ch sp, 3 ch, 6 dc (*UKtr*) into same sp, *2 ch, 7 dc (*UKtr*) into next 3 ch sp*, rep from * to * twice more, 2 ch, join with a sl st to top of 3 ch at beg of round.

Round 3: 4 ch, miss 2 dc (*UKtr*), 1 sc (*UKdc*) into next dc (*UKtr*), 4 ch, miss 2 dc (*UKtr*), 1 sc (*UKdc*) into next dc (*UKtr*), *2 ch, 1 sc (*UKdc*) into next dc (*UKtr*), 4 ch, miss 2 dc (*UKtr*), 1 sc (*UKdc*) into next dc (*UKtr*), 4 ch, miss 2 dc (*UKtr*), 1 sc (*UKdc*) into next dc (*UKtr*)*, rep from * to * twice more, ending last rep with 2 ch, sl st to beg of round. Break B.

Round 4: using C, sl st into first 4 ch sp, 3 ch, 4 dc (*UKtr*) into same 4 ch sp, 3 ch, 5 dc (*UKtr*) into next 4 ch sp, *2 ch, 1 dc (*UKtr*) into sp between groups on round 3, 2 ch, 5 dc (*UKtr*) into next 4 ch sp, 3 ch, 5 dc (*UKtr*) into next 4 ch sp*, rep from * to * twice more, 2 ch, 1 dc (*UKtr*) into sp between groups on round 3, 2 ch, sl st to top of 3 ch at beg of round. Break C.

Round 5: using A, *1 sc (*UKdc*) into each dc (*UKtr*), 2 sc (*UKdc*) into next sp, 1 sc (*UKdc*) into each dc (*UKtr*), 1 sc (*UKdc*) into next sp, 1 sc (*UKdc*) into next dc (*UKtr*), 1 sc (*UKdc*) into next sp*, rep from * to * 3 more times, 1 ch, join with a sl st to beg of round. Fasten off and work in all the ends.

Scalloped Circle

Materials and equipment:

Crochet hook size 3.00mm (US D, UK 10)

DMC Petra 3 crochet cotton – small amounts in each of 3 colours: A, B and C. Alternatively, 1 x 50g ball in each colour will make several scalloped circles.

Motif size:

3½in (9cm) diameter

Instructions:

Using A, make 8 ch, join into a circle with a sl st.

Round 1: 3 ch [counts as first dc (*UKtr*)], work 2 dc (*UKtr*) into ring, leaving the last loop of each dc (*UKtr*) on the hook, now draw the yarn through all loops on the hook, *2 ch, work 3 dc (*UKtr*) into ring, leaving last loop of each dc (*UKtr*) on the hook, yrh, draw the yarn through all 3 loops*, rep from * to * 7 more times, 2 ch, join with a sl st to beg of round (9 clusters in total). Break A.

Round 2: using B, *2 ch, 1 sc (*UKdc*) into next sp, 2 ch, 1sc (*UKdc*) into top of cluster*, rep from * to * all round, 2 ch, join with a sl st to beg of round (18 x 2 ch sp).

Round 3: 6 ch [counts as first dc (*UKtr*) and 3 ch], 1 dc (*UKtr*) into next 2 ch sp, *3 ch, 1 dc (*UKtr*) into next 2 ch sp*, rep from * to * all round, 3 ch, join with a sl st to 3rd ch at beg of round. Break B.

Round 4: using C, *1 sc (*UKdc*) into next sp, 6 dc (*UKtr*) into next sp*, rep from * to * all round, join with a sl st to beg of round. Fasten off and work in all the ends.

Tudor Rose

Materials and equipment:

Crochet hook size 3.00mm (US D, UK 10)

DMC Petra 3 crochet cotton – small amounts in each of 3 colours A, B and C. Alternatively, 1 x 50g ball in each colour will make several of these squares.

For the hand warmers:

Crochet hook size 3.00mm (US D, UK 10)

2 x 50g balls Sirdar Softspun Luxury DK (8-ply), or similar yarn, in turquoise

The hand warmers are 7½in (19cm) long and are designed to fit most women's hands.

Motif size:

3in (7.5cm) diameter

Instructions:

Using A, make 4 ch, join into a circle with a sl st.

Round 1: using A, 3 ch, work 11 dc (*UKtr*) into ring, join to top of 3 ch [12 dc (*UKtr*)]. Break A.

Round 2: using B, *4 ch, 1 sc (*UKdc*) into sp after next 2 dc (*UKtr*)*, rep from * to * all round ending last rep with 1 sl st into first of 4 ch at beg of round [6 x 4 ch sp].

Round 3: sl st into first 4 ch sp, 3 ch, 4 dc (*UKtr*), 3 ch,1 sc (*UKdc*) into same sp, *1 sc (*UKdc*) into next sc (*UKdc*), 1 sc (*UKdc*), 3 ch, 4 dc (*UKtr*), 3 ch,1 sc (*UKdc*) into next 4 ch sp*, rep from * to * all round, ending last rep with 1 sc (*UKdc*) into last sc (*UKdc*).

Round 4: 6 ch, sc (*UKdc*) into centre of next dc (*UKtr*) group, *4 ch, 1 dc (*UKtr*) into next sc (*UKdc*), 4 ch, 1 sc (*UKdc*) into centre of next dc (*UKtr*) group, rep from * to * all round, ending final rep 4 ch, sl st into top of 3rd of 6 ch at beg of round. Break B.

Round 5: using C, sl st into next 4 ch sp, 3 ch, 9 dc (*UKtr*) into same sp, sc (*UKdc*) into next sp, 3 ch, sc (*UKdc*) into next 4 ch sp, *10 dc (*UKtr*) into next 4ch sp, 1 sc (*UKdc*) into next sp, 3 ch, 1 sc (*UKdc*) into next sp*, rep from * to * all round, sl st into top of 3 ch at beg of round. Fasten off and work in all the ends.

To make the hand warmers:

Make 4 squares.

Right hand:

Join two squares together vertically.

Join yarn to the bottom right-hand corner.

Work 34 dc (*UKtr*) along the right edge, working into dc (*UKtr*) and sp across both squares, turn.

Row 1: 3 ch, 1 dc (*UKtr*) into each dc (*UKtr*) to end, turn.

Row 2: 2 ch, 16 hdc (*UKhtr*), 17 dc (*UKtr*), turn.

Row 3: 3 ch, 16 dc (*UKtr*), 17 hdc (*UKhtr*), turn.

Rows 4–8: 3 ch [counts as first dc (*UKtr*)], 1 dc (*UKtr*) into each dc (*UKtr*) to end.

Row 9: 3 ch, 8 dc (*UKtr*), 5 ch, miss 5 dc (*UKtr*), 3 dc (*UKtr*), 17 hdc (*UKhtr*), turn.

Row 10: 2 ch, 16 hdc (*UKhtr*), 3 dc (*UKtr*), 5 dc (*UKtr*) in 5 ch sp, 9 dc (*UKtr*), turn.

Rows 11–12: 3 ch, 1 dc (*UKtr*) into each st to end, turn. Fasten off.

Left hand:

Join two squares together as for right hand.

Join yarn to the top left-hand corner.

Work 34 dc (*UKtr*) along the tops of both squares.

Row 1: 3 ch, 1 dc (*UKtr*) into each dc (*UKtr*) to end, turn.

Row 2: 3 ch, 16 dc (*UKtr*), 17 hdc (*UKhtr*), turn.

Row 3: 2 ch, 16 hdc (*UKhtr*), 17 dc (*UKtr*).

Rows 4–8: 3 ch [counts as first dc (*UKtr*)], 1 dc (*UKtr*) into each dc (*UKtr*) to end.

Row 9: 2 ch, 16 hdc (*UKhtr*), 3 dc (*UKtr*), 5 ch, miss 5 dc (*UKtr*), 9 dc (*UKtr*), turn.

Row 10: 3 ch, 8 dc (*UKtr*), 5 dc (*UKtr*) into 5 ch sp, 3 dc (*UKtr*), 17 hdc (*UKhtr*), turn.

Rows 11–12: 3 ch, 1 dc (*UKtr*) into each st to end, turn. Fasten off.

Edging:

With right side facing, rejoin yarn to top edge, work 1 row of sc (*UKdc*) all along, turn.

Next row: *1 dc (*UKtr*) into next sc (*UKdc*), 1 sl st into next sc (*UKdc*)*, rep from * to * across row. Fasten off.

Rejoin yarn to bottom edge and work across sts in exactly the same way.

Work in the ends and sew the seams.

Catherine Wheel

Materials and equipment:

Crochet hook size 3.00mm (US D, UK 10)

DMC Petra 3 crochet cotton – small amounts in each of 3 colours: A, B and C. Alternatively, 1 x 50g ball in each colour will make several of these squares.

Motif size:

4in (10cm) diameter

Instructions:

Using A, make 6 ch, join into a circle with a sl st.

Round 1: using A, 1 ch, work 12 sc (UKdc) into circle, join with a sl st.

Round 2: using B, 3 ch, 1 dc (UKtr) into same sp, leave last loop on hook, draw through both loops, 2 ch, *2 dc (UKtr) into next dc, leaving last loop on hook, yrh, draw through both loops, 2 ch*, rep from * to * all round, joining to top of first dc (UKtr) at beg of round. Break B.

Round 3: using C, sl st into first 2 ch, 1 sc (UKdc) into sp, 3 ch,1 sc (UKdc) into next sp, *3 ch, 1 sc (UKdc) into next sp*, rep from * to * all round, 3 ch, sl st to beg of round.

Round 4: using C, sl st into first 3 ch sp, 3 ch, 2 dc (UKtr) into same sp, leaving last loop on hook, yrh, draw through all loops on hook, *4 ch, 3 dc (UKtr) into next sp, leaving last loop on hook, yrh, draw through all loops*, rep from * to * all round, join with a sl st to top of 3 ch at beg of round. Break C.

Round 5: using A, sl st into next 4 ch sp, 3 ch, 3 dc (UKtr) into same sp, 3 ch, 4 dc (UKtr) into same sp, *1 ch, 4 dc (UKtr) into next sp, 1 ch, 4 dc (UKtr) into next sp, 1 ch, [4 dc (UKtr), 3 ch, 4 dc (UKtr)] into next sp*, rep from * to * twice more, 1 ch, 4 dc (UKtr) into next sp, 1 ch, 4 dc (UKtr) into next sp, 1 ch, join with a sl st to dc (UKtr) at beg of round. Break A.

Round 6: using B, 1 sc (UKdc) into each dc (UKtr) all round and 4 sc (UKdc) into each corner sp, join with a sl st to beg of round. Fasten off and work in all the ends.

Circle in a Square

Materials and equipment:

Crochet hook size 3.00mm (US D, UK 10)

DMC Petra 3 crochet cotton – small amounts in each of 3 colours: A, B and C. Alternatively, 1 x 50g ball in each colour will make several of these squares.

Motif size:

2½in (6.5cm) diameter

Instructions:

Using A, make 6 ch, join into a circle with a sl st.

Round 1: work 12 sc (*UKdc*) into circle, join with a sl st to beg of round. Break A.

Round 2: using B, 3 ch, 1dc (*UKtr*) into the same sp, *2 ch, 2 dc (*UKtr*) into next sc (*UKdc*)*, rep from * to * all round, ending 2 ch, sl st to top of 3 ch at beg of round. Break B.

Round 3: using C, 1 sc (*UKdc*) into next 2 ch sp, *4 ch, 1 sc (*UKdc*) into next 2 ch sp*, rep from * to * all round, ending last rep with 4 ch, sl st to beg of round.

Round 4: sl st into next 4 ch sp, 3 ch, 3 dc (*UKtr*), 3 ch, 4 dc (*UKtr*) into same sp, *2 ch, 1 sc (*UKdc*) into next sp, 2 ch, 1 sc (*UKdc*) into next sp, 2 ch, 4 dc (*UKtr*), 2 ch, 4 dc (*UKtr*) into next sp*, rep from * to * twice more, ending last rep with 2 ch, 1 sc (*UKdc*) into next sp, 2 ch, 1 sc (*UKdc*) into next sp, 2 ch, sl st into dc (*UKtr*) at beg of round. Fasten off and work in all the ends.

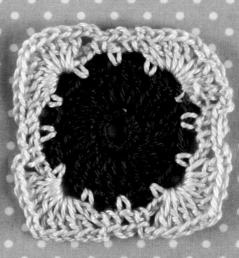

Floral Ring

Materials and equipment:

Crochet hook size 3.00mm (US D, UK 10)

DMC Petra 3 crochet cotton – small amounts in each of 4 colours A, B, C and D. Alternatively, 1 x 50g ball in each colour will make several of these circles.

For the pincushion:

Crochet hook size 3.00mm (US D, UK 10)

DMC Petra 3 crochet cotton – small amounts in each of 4 colours A, B, C and D

Small piece of matching cotton fabric

Small amount of fibrefill stuffing

Matching thread and sewing needle

Motif size:

4¼in (11cm) diameter

Instructions:

Using A, make 12 ch, join into a ring with a sl st.

Round 1: work 3 ch, 31 dc (*UKtr*) into ring, join with a sl st to beg of round [32 dc (*UKtr*)]. Break A.

Round 2: using B, work 4 ch, 2 dc (*UKtr*) into 3rd ch from hook, *miss 1 dc (*UKtr*), 1 tr (*UKdtr*) into next ch, 2 dc (*UKtr*) into centre of tr (*UKdtr*)*, rep from * to * 14 more times, join to top of 4 ch. Break B.

Round 3: using C, work 3 ch, 1 dc (*UKtr*) into each of the next 2 dc (*UKtr*), keeping the last loop of each dc (*UKtr*) on the hook (3 loops on hook), yrh, draw yarn through all 3 loops, *work 4 ch, 1 dc (*UKtr*) into each of next 3 dc (*UKtr*), keeping the last loop of each dc (*UKtr*) on the hook, yrh, draw yarn through all loops on hook*, rep from * to * all round, ending with 4 ch, join to top of first dc (*UKtr*) in round. Break C.

Round 4: using D, work 1 ch, 4 sc (*UKdc*) into next sp, 1 sc (*UKdc*) into top of cluster, 3 ch, sl st into 3rd ch from hook, *4 sc (*UKdc*) into next sp, 1 sc (*UKdc*) into top of next cluster, 3 ch, sl st into 3rd ch from hook*, rep from * to * all round, join with a sl st to beg of round. Fasten off and work in all the ends.

To make the pincushion:

Make 2 motifs. Using a motif as a template, cut 2 circles of fabric slightly bigger than the motif, thus leaving enough fabric to form the seam. With wrong sides of the fabric facing, sew a seam by hand or on a sewing machine all round the circle, leaving a small opening to turn and stuff the pincushion. Turn the fabric lining right side out and press lightly to form a neat circle. Stuff the cushion firmly and then close the opening with a few concealed stitches. Place the 2 motifs together and join them by sewing the tips of the picots together all round the motif. Leave a gap and slip the cushion into the crocheted cover. Arrange the cushion neatly then close up the gap.

Circle & Shell Square

Materials and equipment:

Crochet hook size 3.00mm (US D, UK 10)

DMC Petra 3 crochet cotton – small
amounts in each of 3 colours: A, B
and C. Alternatively, 1 x 50g ball in
each colour will make several of these
squares.

Motif size:

2in (5cm) diameter

Instructions:

Using A, make 7 ch, join into a circle with a sl st.

Round 1: 3 ch, work 15 dc (*UKtr*) into circle, join with a sl st to top
of 3 ch at beg of round. Break A.

Round 2: using B, 4 ch, miss 1 dc (*UKtr*), *7 dc (*UKtr*) into next dc
(*UKtr*), 1 ch, miss 1 dc (*UKtr*), 1 dc (*UKtr*) into next dc (*UKtr*), 1 ch,
miss 1 dc (*UKtr*)*, rep from * to * twice more, ending last rep with
7 dc (*UKtr*) into next dc (*UKtr*), 1 ch, miss 1 dc (*UKtr*), sl st into 3rd
of 4 ch at beg of round. Break B.

Round 3: using C, *1 sc (*UKdc*) into next sp, 1 sc (*UKdc*) into each
of next 3 dc (*UKtr*), 3 dc (*UKtr*) into next dc (*UKtr*) [at the corner], 1
sc (*UKdc*) into each of next 3 dc (*UKtr*), 1 sc (*UKdc*) into next sp, 1
sc (*UKdc*) into next dc (*UKtr*)*, rep from * to * all round, join with a
sl st to beg of round. Fasten off and work in all the ends.

Daisy Loop

Materials and equipment:

Crochet hook size 3.00mm (US D, UK 10)

DMC Petra 3 crochet cotton – small amounts in each of 3 colours A, B and C. Alternatively, 1 x 50g ball in each colour will make several of these squares.

For the scarf:

Crochet hook size 4.00mm (US G, UK 8)

Rowan Classic Kid aran-weight (10-ply) or similar yarn:
    1 x 50g ball in pale pink (A)
    3 x 50g balls in cream (B)
    2 x 50g balls in pale blue (C)
    1 x 50g ball in burgundy (D)

Size: 61in (155cm) long and 5in (13cm) wide

Motif size:

3¼in (8cm) diameter

Instructions:

Using A, make 6 ch, join into a circle with a sl st.

Round 1: 1 ch, work 12 sc (UKdc) into circle, join with a sl st. Break A.

Round 2: using B, *13 ch, 1 sc (UKdc) into next sc (UKdc)*, rep from * to * 10 more times, 13 ch, sl st into first sc (UKdc) at beg of round (12 petals). Break B.

Round 3: join in C to any petal with a sl st, 3 ch, 2 dc (UKtr) into same sp, leaving last loop of each st on the hook, 3 loops on hook, yrh, draw yarn through all loops, 3 ch, 3 dc (UKtr) into same sp but leaving last loop of each st on hook, yrh, draw yarn through all loops on hook [3 dc (UKtr) cluster formed], *3 ch, 1 sc (UKdc) into next sp, 3 ch, 1 sc (UKdc) into next sp, 3 ch, [3 dc (UKtr) cluster, 3 ch, 3 dc (UKtr) cluster] into next sp*, rep from * to * 3 times, 3 ch, 1 sc (UKdc) into next loop, 3 ch, 1 sc (UKdc) into next loop, 3 ch, sl st to top of first cluster. Break C.

Round 4: join in A, sl st to centre of next 3 ch sp, 3 ch, 3 dc (UKtr) into same sp, but leaving last loop of each dc (UKtr) on hook, yrh, draw yarn through all loops on hook, 4 ch, 4 dc (UKtr) into next sp, leaving last loop of each st on hook, yrh, draw yarn through all loops on hook [4 dc (UKtr) cluster made], *3 ch, 1 sc (UKdc) into next sp, 3 ch, 3 dc (UKtr) cluster into next sp, 3 ch, 1 sc (UKdc) into next sp, 3 ch, [4 dc (UKtr) cluster, 4 ch, 4 dc (UKtr) cluster] into next sp*, rep from * to * 3 times, 3 ch, 1 sc (UKdc) into next sp, 3 ch, 3 dc (UKtr) cluster into next sp, 3 ch, 1 sc (UKdc) into next sp, 3 ch, sl st to top of cluster at beg of round. Fasten off and work in all the ends.

To make the scarf:

Make 13 squares, 7 using A for the starting ch and Round 1, and 6 using D for the starting ch and Round 1. Work Rounds 2 and 4 in cream and Round 3 in pale blue. Work in all the ends. Sew the squares together in a row, alternating the coloured centres.

Edging:

Using B and the 4.00mm (US G, UK 8) crochet hook, join the yarn to one corner of the scarf with a sl st. Work 6 dc (UKtr) into the corner of the motif, then work along the motifs as follows:

1 sc (UKdc) into next sc (UKdc), 1 ch, 6 dc (UKtr) into top of next cluster, 1 ch, 1 sc (UKdc) into next sc (UKdc), 1 ch, 6 dc (UKtr) into the point where the two squares have been sewn together, rep from * to * all round the scarf, but working 6 dc (UKtr), 3 ch, 6 dc (UKtr) into each corner sp, and ending last rep with 6 dc (UKtr) into last corner, 3 ch, join with a sl st to top of first dc (UKtr) at beg of round.

Pinwheel Circle

Materials and equipment:

Crochet hook size 3.00mm (US D, UK 10)

DMC Petra 3 crochet cotton – small
amounts in each of 3 colours:
A, B and C. Alternatively,
1 x 50g ball in each colour
will make several of these
squares.

Motif size:

4in (10cm) diameter

Instructions:

Using A, make 10 ch, join with a sl st to form a ring.

Round 1: , 3 ch, work 31 dc (*UKtr*) into ring, join with a sl st to 3
ch at beg of round. Break A.

Round 2: using B, *4 ch, 1 sc (*UKdc*) into 4th dc (*UKtr*)*, rep all
round , joining last rep to base of 4 ch at beg of round.

Round 3: using B, sl st into first sp, 4 ch, 5 dc (*UKtr*) into first sp,
*1 ch, 6 dc (*UKtr*) into next sp*, rep from * to * all round, join last
rep to top of 4 ch at beg of round. Break B.

Round 4: using C, *6 ch, 1 sc (*UKdc*) into sp between groups*,
rep from * to * all round, join to top of 6 ch at beg of round.

Round 5: using C, sl st into first 6 ch sp, 3 ch, 5 dc (*UKtr*), 3 ch,
6 dc (*UKtr*) into next 6 ch sp, *1 ch, 6 dc (*UKtr*) into next 6 ch sp,
1 ch, [6 dc (*UKtr*), 3 ch, 6 dc (*UKtr*)] into next sp*, rep from * to *
twice more, 1 ch, 6 dc (*UKtr*) into next 6 ch sp, 1 ch, sl st to top of
3 ch at beg of round. Fasten off and work in all the ends.

Dog Rose Triangle

Materials and equipment:

Crochet hook size 3.00mm (US D, UK 10)

DMC Petra 3 crochet cotton – small amounts in each of 3 colours A, B and C. Alternatively, 1 x 50g ball in each colour will make several of these triangles.

For the mat:

Crochet hook size 3.00mm (US D, UK 10)

DMC Petra 3 crochet cotton – small amounts in a variety of colours, including light and dark green

Motif size:

3in (7.5cm) from point to point.

Instructions:

Using A, make 4 ch, join into a circle with a sl st.

Round 1: 3 ch, work 11 dc (*UKtr*) into ring, join with a sl st to top of 3 ch at beg of round. Break A.

Round 2: using B, 5 ch [counts as dc (*UKtr*) and 2 ch], miss 1 dc (*UKtr*), *4 dc (*UKtr*) cluster in next dc (*UKtr*), 2 ch, 1 dc (*UKtr*) into next dc (*UKtr*), 2 ch*, rep from * to * ending last rep with 2 ch, sl st to 3rd of 5 ch at beg of round. Break B.

Round 3: using C, 1 sc (*UKdc*) into next 2 ch sp, 1 ch, *[5 dc (*UKtr*), 6 ch, work 1 sl st into 3rd ch from hook (picot made), 3 ch, 5 dc (*UKtr*)] into the top of next cluster, 1 sc (*UKdc*) into next sp, 2 ch, 1 sc (*UKdc*) into top of next cluster, 2 ch, 1 sc (*UKdc*) into next sp, 2 ch*, rep from * to * twice more, sl st to beg of round. Fasten off and work in all the ends.

To make the mat:

Make 6 triangles in whatever colours you choose. Sew them together as in the photograph.

Edging:

Join light green to any corner, work in sc (*UKdc*) evenly all round mat [approximately 24 sc (*UKdc*) across each motif]. Join with a sl st to beg of round. Work one more round in light green, working 3 sc (*UKdc*) into each of the 6 corner sts to keep the work flat. Join with a sl st as before. Break light green. Join in dark green and work a further round of sc (*UKdc*), working 3 sc (*UKdc*) into the corner sts as before. Fasten off.

Picot Hexagon

Materials and equipment:

Crochet hook size 3.00mm (US D, UK 10)

DMC Petra 3 crochet cotton – small amounts in each of 4 colours: A, B, C and D. Alternatively, 1 x 50g ball in each colour will make several hexagons.

Motif size:

3½in (9cm) diameter

Instructions:

Using A, make 6 ch, join into a ring with a sl st.

Round 1: work 1 ch, 12 sc (*UKdc*) into ring, join.

Round 2: work 1 ch, 2 sc (*UKdc*) into each sc (*UKdc*) to end. Break A.

Round 3: using B, work 3 ch, 3 dc (*UKtr*) into same ch as join, *4 ch, miss 3 sc (*UKdc*), 4 dc (*UKtr*) into next sc (*UKdc*)*, rep from * to * all round, ending with 4 ch, join to top of 3 ch at beg of round [6 x 4 dc (*UKtr*) groups]. Break B.

Round 4: using C, work 3 ch, 1 dc (*UKtr*) into each of next 3 dc (*UKtr*), but leaving last loop of each st on hook, yrh, draw loop through all loops on hook, *5 ch, 1 sc (*UKdc*) into 4 ch loop, 5 ch**, 1 dc (*UKtr*) into each of next 4 dc (*UKtr*), leaving last loop of each dc (*UKtr*) on hook, yrh, draw loop through all loops on hook*. Rep from * to * all round but ending last rep at **. Join with a sl st to top of 4 dc (*UKtr*) group at beg of round. Break C.

Round 5: using D, in same place as sl st make 3 ch, work a sl st into 4th ch from hook (picot made), *4 sc (*UKdc*) into next 5 ch loop, 1 sc (*UKdc*) into next sc (*UKdc*), 4 sc (*UKdc*) into next 5 ch loop**, 1 sc (*UKdc*) into top of group, 3 ch, sl st into 3rd ch from hook (picot made)*, rep from * to * all round, ending last rep at **, sl st to top of first group, fasten off. Work in all the ends neatly.

Alpine Meadow Square

Materials and equipment:

Crochet hook size 3.00mm (US D, UK 10)

DMC Petra 3 crochet cotton – small amounts in each of 3 colours A, B and C. Alternatively, 1 x 50g ball in each colour will make several of these squares.

For the shoulder bag:

Crochet hook size 3.00mm (US D, UK 10)

DMC Petra 3 crochet cotton – small amounts in various colours including light and dark green, and 1 x 50g ball in ecru.

Motif size:

3½in (9cm) diameter

Instructions:

Using A, make 2 ch, 6 sc (*UKdc*) into 2nd ch from hook, join.

Round 1: 1 ch, 2 sc (*UKdc*) into each sc (*UKdc*) to end, join.

Round 2: as round 1. Break A.

Round 3: using B, 4 ch, 3 tr (*UKdtr*) into same sp, leaving last loop of each st on hook, yrh, draw yarn through all loops on hook, *3 ch, miss 1 sc (*UKdc*), 4 tr (*UKdtr*) into next sc (*UKdc*), leaving last loop of each st on hook, yrh, draw through all loops on hook*, rep from * to * 10 more times, end last rep 3 ch, join with a sl st to top of 4 ch at beg of round. Break B.

Round 4: using C, sl st into first 3ch sp, 2 dc (*UKtr*), 4 ch, 3dc (*UKtr*) in same sp, *1 dc (*UKtr*) into next sp, 2 ch, 1 dc (*UKtr*) into next sp, 2 ch, 3 dc (*UKtr*), 4 ch, 3 dc (*UKtr*) into next 3 ch sp, 2 ch*, rep from * to * all round, sl st into top of 3 ch at beg of round.

Round 5: sl st into next sp, 1 ch, *4 sc (*UKdc*), 2 ch, 4 sc (*UKdc*) into same sp, 3 ch, 1 dc (*UKtr*) round stem of dc (*UKtr*) of previous round, 3 ch, 1 dc (*UKtr*) round stem of dc (*UKtr*) of previous round, 3 ch*, rep from * to * all round, join to top of 3 ch at beg of round. Fasten off and work in all the ends.

To make the shoulder bag:

Make 8 squares, 4 with Round 4 worked in dark green and 4 with Round 4 worked in light green, and using various colours for each floral motif. Work in all the ends.

Join the squares in 2 strips of 4, alternating the light and dark green backgrounds.

Centre strip:

Using ecru, join the yarn to a top corner on one of the strips. Work in sc (*UKdc*) along the long edge [70 sc (*UKdc*) in total], turn.

Row 1: 1 ch, work 1 sc (*UKdc*) into each sc (*UKdc*) all along the row, turn.

Repeat row 1 nine more times, fasten off.

Side strips:

Rejoin the yarn to the other top corner on the same 4-square strip.

Work 70 sc (*UKdc*) along the long edge as before, Turn.

Row 1: 1 ch, work 1 sc (*UKdc*) into each sc (*UKdc*) all along the row, turn.

Repeat row 1 four more times, fasten off.

Take the other 4-square strip and rejoin the yarn to the top corner on what will be the outer edge. Work as for the other side strip. Fasten off.

To make up:

Join the two pieces of work together along the centre strip. Fold in half widthwise and join the side seams.

Top edging:

Rejoin the yarn to one side seam at the top of the bag, 1 ch, work a round of sc (*UKdc*) all round the bag, join to beg of round with a sl st. Work a further 5 rounds in sc (*UKdc*), joining as before on each round. Fasten off.

Strap:

Using ecru, make 11 ch, 1 sc (*UKdc*) into 2nd ch from hook, 1 sc (*UKdc*) into each ch to end, turn.

Row 1: 1 ch, work 1 sc (*UKdc*) into each sc (*UKdc*) to end, turn.

Rows 2–8: work as row 1.

Row 9: 3 ch [counts as first dc (*UKtr*)], 1 dc (*UKtr*) into each sc (*UKdc*) to end, turn.

Rows 10–13: work as row 9.

Repeat the last 13 rows until strap measures 32in (81cm) ending on an 8th row. Fasten off Sew the strap to each side of the bag.

Autumn Square

Materials and equipment:

Crochet hook size 3.00mm (US D, UK 10)

DMC Petra 3 crochet cotton – small amounts in each of 3 colours: A, B and C. Alternatively, 1 x 50g ball in each colour will make several of these squares.

Motif size:

3in (7.5cm) diameter

Instructions:

Using A, make 4 ch and join into a circle with a sl st.

Round 1: 5 ch [counts as 1 dc (*UKtr*) and 2 ch], *1 dc (*UKtr*), 2 ch into ring*, rep from * to * 11 times, join to 3 ch at beg of round. Break A.

Round 2: using B, 3 ch, 2 dc (*UKtr*), leaving last loop of each st on hook, yrh and draw through all loops [3 dc (*UKtr*) cluster made], *3 ch, 3 dc (*UKtr*) cluster into 2 ch sp*, rep from * to * all round, ending last rep with 2 ch, sl st to top of 3 ch at beg of round. Break B.

Round 3: using C, sl st into first 2 ch sp, *1 sc (*UKdc*) into sp, 4 ch*, rep from * to * all round, sl st into sc (*UKdc*) at beg of round.

Round 4: *5 dc (*UKtr*), 3 ch, 5 dc (*UKtr*) into next 4 ch sp, 1 sc (*UKdc*) into next 4 ch sp, 3 ch, 1 sc (*UKdc*) into next 4 ch sp*, rep from * to * 3 more times, sl st to dc (*UKtr*) at beg of round. Fasten off and work in all the ends.

Filet Heart

Materials and equipment:

Crochet hook size 3.00mm
(US D, UK 10)

DMC Petra 3 crochet cotton in
colour of your choice

For the baby blanket:

Crochet hook size 4.00mm
(US G, UK 8)

Sirdar Snuggly DK (8-ply) or
similar yarn:

1 x 50g ball each in pale blue,
lemon, pale pink and mint
green; 3 x 50g balls in white

The blanket measures
approximately 25½in (65cm)
wide and 28in (71cm) deep

Motif size:

4½in (11.5cm) diameter

Instructions:

This square is worked in filet
crochet. It is charted in squares
where each vertical line on the chart
represents 1 dc (*UKtr*) and each horizontal line
represents 1 ch. Where a square is filled, work 1
dc (*UKtr*) instead of 1 ch.

Row 1: make 30 ch, 1 dc (*UKtr*) into 3rd ch from
hook, 1 dc (*UKtr*) into each ch to end, turn.

Row 2: 3 ch, 1 dc (*UKtr*) into next dc (*UKtr*),
*1 ch, miss 1 dc (*UKtr*), 1 dc (*UKtr*) in next dc
(*UKtr*)*, rep
from * to * to last 3 dc
(*UKtr*), 1 ch, miss 1 dc (*UKtr*), 1 dc (*UKtr*) in each
of last 2 dc (*UKtr*).

Continue to work from the chart until all rows
are worked. Fasten off and work in all the ends.

To make the baby blanket:

The blanket is worked as 4 vertical strips of 5
squares. The sequence of colours, from right to
left, that I have used for each strip is:

Strip A: green, white, pink, white, green.

Strip B: white, blue, white, yellow, white.

Strip C: pink, white, green, white, pink.

Strip D: white, yellow, white, blue, white.

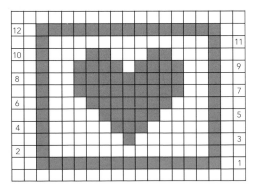

To achieve the white strip in between the coloured squares, work the following rows in white: row 12 of the first square in each strip; rows 1 and 12 of the second, third and fourth squares; and row 1 of the fifth square.

When you have completed all the squares, work the ends in on each one and lay them out on a flat surface in the correct pattern. Carefully sew them together, matching them row for row to maintain a uniform shape.

Edging:

Rejoin the white yarn to one corner of the blanket. Work a row of sc (*UKdc*) all round the edges, working into each st across the top and bottom and each row end along both sides. Join with a sl st to beg of round.

Next round: 1 ch, work 1 sc (*UKdc*) into each sc (*UKdc*) all round but work 3 sc (*UKdc*) into each corner as you reach it. Join as before.

Next round: work as previous round, but working 3 sc (*UKdc*) into centre sc (*UKdc*) of each corner.

Next round: as previous round.

Next round: 1 ch, then work a round of sc (*UKdc*) from left to right instead, thus creating a twisted edging (crab stitch), join as before with a sl st. Fasten off. Work in any loose ends.

Acknowledgements

My thanks go, as always, to Search Press for their never-ending
help and support, fantastic editing and fabulous photography
that all go towards the making of my lovely books.
Many thanks also to DMC, Patons, Rowan Yarns
and Sirdar for supporting me with their yarns.
And last but by no means least, a big thank you
to all my family and friends for their help,
advice and support.

Publisher's Note

If you would like more information
about crocheting, try the
Beginner's Guide to Crochet
by Pauline Turner,
Search Press, 2005.